"Written for 'proclaimers' of the Word for all ages—children, youth, adults, parish ministers, parents, and family groups—these prayer services celebrate the seasons, prayer, sacraments, peace and justice, and the life of a contemporary Christian....The rituals are beautifully simple and adaptable to any particular situation for effective communal prayer experiences. Parents especially would find the individual services delightful for use with family prayer times since children and adults can participate with ease in sharing, praying, and responding to the Word of God."

Juanita Allen
Modern Liturgy

"Composed and arranged by Gwen Costello, who has had many years of experience teaching religion, these prayer services are grouped under four headings: for children, for pre-teens and teenagers, for catechists, and for parents and family groups.

"What is most helpful is that none of the materials used are expensive or difficult to obtain and each service is brief. Any group that uses these services could easily become more prayerful and more active Christians."

Msgr. Charles Diviney
The Tablet

"This work stresses the importance of a real day-to-day connection between God and believing Christians, nurtured by a practical experience of prayer. The 32 prayer services in the book address such areas as liturgical feasts, contemporary concerns, and faith topics useful to prayer leaders. Each inspiring service includes a section on how to prepare for it. Catechists, lay ministers, and parish leaders will much appreciate the insightful and timely concerns in the book."

Book World

"Thirty-two short prayer services that beautifully address areas such as liturgical feasts, contemporary concerns, and other faith topics useful to lay prayer leaders....the 'proclaimers' who lead these services can be of any age. The services are brief and inspiring. There are music suggestions, as well as ideas for other activities to create and enhance an atmosphere of prayer. The services for children can be used in the classroom, before special events, or in a home setting. Also, the services for teens and pre-teens are adaptable to a variety of situations, and address concerns helpful to the developing faith life of this age group."

Doctrine and Life

GWEN COSTELLO

PRAYER SERVICES

F·O·R

Religious Educators

TWENTY-THIRD PUBLICATIONS
Mystic, Connecticut

Also by Gwen Costello

A Bible Way of the Cross for Children

Stations of the Cross for Teenagers

Praying with Children

A Way of the Cross for Religion Teachers

Third printing 1990

Twenty-Third Publications
185 Willow Street
PO Box 180'
Mystic CT   06355
(203) 536-2611

ISBN: 0-89622-390-6
Library of Congress Catalog Card Number: 88-051811

The illustrations are reproduced by courtesy of
Liturgical Publications, Inc., Brookfield, Wisconsin.

Contents

FOR CATECHISTS AND OTHER PARISH MINISTERS

FOR PARENTS AND FAMILY GROUPS

Introduction

This is a book for people who share faith with others in group settings. This is a resource for proclaimers. An important, even essential, aspect of Christian proclamation is prayer. We share faith as much through our expression of it in prayer as through what we say "about" it—maybe even more so. When we can combine the two, when our prayer also teaches us something about our faith, we are doubly blessed.

The services in this book are an attempt to offer "double blessings." They offer complete prayer experiences that also teach valuable faith lessons. In every case participants are involved in some manner so that they can respond to God in realistic, practical ways. Many of the services, especially those for the young, offer hands-on activities that involve the whole person. The point is, prayer is a real experience that relates to our lives here and now. God exists and reaches out to us. God is with us in all our life experiences. We reach back toward God when we share this belief with one another and express it through prayer.

All of these services can be used in a variety of religious education settings: in homes, classrooms, churches, or meeting rooms. The faith of the believers is what makes any setting a sacred place. And they can be used with "proclaimers" of all ages: preschoolers, elementary children, pre-teens, teenagers, or adults. And by people with diverse roles in religious education: parents, catechists, teachers, priests, or DREs. Some of these services are geared directly toward children and some toward youth and adults, but all can be adapted to almost any catechetical group in any parish program.

Every moment of our religious education ministry can be celebrated in prayer: new beginnings, Halloween, All Saints, Advent, Christmas, Lent, Easter, Pentecost, Ordinary time, and sacrament preparation. In this book you will find a service to celebrate each of these moments—and more. There are services to celebrate faith, to build peace, to establish harmony, to reflect on our role as Christians, to focus on the act of praying itself.

Use these services often, and adapt them to your own particular groups and/or situations. Let them inspire you to develop your own, highly personal, prayer services. Involve parents, catechists and teachers, even the children and teenagers themselves, in creating words and rituals that express the process of learning about and loving God that you as a group experience. It doesn't really matter which words and rituals you use; the important thing is to pray together often. My hope is that these services will be a starting point as you continue to proclaim God's presence among you.

FOR CHILDREN

1   *Learning to Pray*

To Prepare   Have one 2"x2" piece of paper for each child, on which are printed these three words: *Think, Pray, Listen,* as well as each child's name. On your prayer table, place a candle and a bowl in which to place the slips of paper. As the children arrive, invite them to sit on the floor in a circle around the prayer table.

Leader   Children, God is always with us. Sometimes we speak to God and sometimes God speaks to us. When we speak to God, our words are called prayer. I invite you now to pray with me. Together, let us think about God, speak to God, and listen quietly for God to speak to us.

Time to Think
(Ask the children to think about the following questions. Allow a brief moment of silence between each.)

•Who made you?
•Who cares about you every minute of the day and night?
•Who gave you the special gift of laughter?
•Who loves you just the way you are?

(Now invite verbal responses to these questions. Many children will answer "my mother or father." Explain that parents are another gift from God.)

Time to Pray
(Ask the children to think of something in their lives they particularly like. Then, invite each, in turn, to say the following aloud: "Thank you, God, for _____." Be sure to also take a turn yourself.)

Time to Listen
(Demonstrate to the children several bodily gestures they can use to speak to God in their hearts and to listen.

For example, folding hands, bowing head, closing eyes, kneeling. Allow them to choose the posture that appeals to them. Invite them to assume that posture and to remain silent for a minute or so.)

Leader God made us and God loves us very much. To remind us that we can speak to God and also listen to God anytime we want, I have here a special message for each of you.

(Pick up the slips one by one. Call each child forward to receive his or her slip. Invite them to take these slips home and put them where they will see them often.)

2 *And It Was Good*

To Prepare   Cut out 6"x1" strips of colored paper, one piece for each participant. Place these strips in a special container. Also have available a roll of magic tape. Invite participants to stand in a circle. In the center of the circle place the container with the paper strips.

Leader   (The following story is an adaptation of the creation story in Genesis. Read or tell it slowly and with great expression.) In the beginning God made this world, and when everything was finished, God thought that the world was good. Every animal and bird that God created got along with every other animal and bird. The trees and flowers, the rivers and seas, the sun and the moon, all were made by God, and there was peace and harmony among them. Each understood what its role was and each did it.

Into this world of peace and harmony, God placed a man and a woman. They loved God's beautiful world, but they made foolish decisions. They decided to do things their way, to follow a path different from the one God made for them. Soon the peace and harmony of God's world was interrupted. People began to fight and to be jealous of one another.

Many years later, Jesus came into this world. Jesus believed that peace and harmony should be restored, so that our world would be as God intended it to be. Jesus taught his followers to live in peace and harmony.

We are followers of Jesus. We can live in peace with one another, and we can work to restore peace to our world. We can do this together and we can share this message with others.

Leader How do you think we can help to restore peace and harmony to our beautiful world?

(Invite the children to suggest ways this might be done. After the discussion, invite each child to go to the center of the circle and take a colored strip. Finally, you take a strip. Attach your strip end-to-end with a piece of tape. Turn to the child on your right and ask him or her to place his or her strip inside yours and then tape it end-to-end. Proceed around the circle until all the strips are attached in a colorful paper chain. Spread out this completed chain in the center of the group.)

Leader God, our beloved parent, thank you for our world. Help us to work hard to restore the peace and harmony you want for us. We offer you this peace chain as a sign of our willingness to work together. Let it remind us that each of us must do our part to restore peace on earth. To this we say "Amen."

All Amen.

3   *Living Together in Peace*

To Prepare   Make a small card for each child, on which is printed the following: *Peace: Oh, how good it is!* Invite the children to sit in a circle on the floor.

Leader   Let us join hands as we pray: Thank you, God, for creating our world.

All   Thank you, God, for creating our world.

Leader   Thank you, God, for creating us.

All   Thank you, God, for creating us.

Leader   Teach us how to live together in·peace.

All   Teach us how to live together in peace.

Leader   Help us to restore peace to our world.

All   Help us to restore peace to our world.

Leader   Amen.

All   Amen.

(After this opening prayer, ask the children the following questions: What is peace? What does peace mean for you? See if you can, as a group, reach some common understanding about what kind of "peace" you want to restore to our world. After the discussion, continue as follows.)

Leader   Today we're going to learn a song about peace. Once we learn it, we'll be able to sing it together. It goes like this. (Teach the song line by line. It's sung to the tune of "Old MacDonald Had a Farm.")

God, our Creator, made this world.
Oh, how good it is.
In this world God wanted peace.
Oh, how good it is.
With peace, peace here and peace, peace there
Here peace, there peace, everywhere peace, peace,
God, our Creator, made this world.
Oh, how good it is.

(Allow sufficient time for the children to practice the song. When most of them know it, stand for the closing ritual.)

Leader   Let us now sing together our class peace song. (After the song, get the cards you have prepared beforehand and call the children forward, one by one, to receive them. As you present them, say the following:——————, remember our class song, and work hard for peace.)

Child   Amen.

4   *Jesus Is Our Light*

To Prepare   This short prayer service can be used in the classroom or at church during a children's Halloween liturgy or paraliturgy. Invite children to wear their costumes for the service. On the prayer table, place an unlit candle beside a jack-o-lantern. Allow the children to take the readers' parts.

First Reader   Tonight is a very special night, one of our favorite nights of the year because it's lots of fun. We wear our costumes and walk around with our family and friends to ask for Halloween treats, like candy, fruit, and popcorn.

Second Reader   Because it's dark when we go out, we need a light to guide us. Some people carry flashlights and some people carry jack-o-lanterns to light their way.

Third Reader   We should remember when we go out this evening that we also have another kind of light to guide us. Jesus, who is the Light of the World, will be with us. We should ask Jesus to guide us as we travel from house to house.

Leader   (Light the candle and place it inside the jack-o-lantern.) Jesus, please bless this jack-o-lantern which reminds us that we need light to guide us in the darkness. Help us to remember this evening that you are with us. You are our very special light. (Now ask the children to step forward, one at a time, to describe their costumes. They might say something like: "I am a princess," or "My name is Frankenstein." After they announce who they are, offer the following individual blessings.)

Leader   (While forming the Sign of the Cross on each child's forehead)————————, dressed as a princess, may Jesus bless you and watch over you on this Halloween night. ————————, dressed as Frankenstein....

Child Amen.

(After all the children have been blessed, invite them to join hands and recite the Our Father.)

5   *We Are Saints, Too*

To Prepare   For this service, invite children to dress up as their name saint or a favorite saint, or, at least, to bring to class something that represents this person. You may want to send a note home to parents explaining what you are doing, so that the children won't forget their costume or symbol on the appointed day. Choose some lively music for the closing procession.

Leader   We are all children of God. God made us and God loves us more than we'll ever know. Saints are people who love God back. They try to show, by the way they live, that God is important to them. They spend time talking to God in prayer. Some of us have been named for saints, and many of us have a favorite saint. Let us take turns now calling out the names of our special saints and let us ask them to help us to be saints, too. (The leader should call out the name of a saint to begin this process. For example, Saint Agnes. All respond: "Teach us to follow Jesus." Continue until each child has named a saint.)

(Now invite the children to come forward, one at a time, to show something or say something about their patron or favorite saint. When all have had a turn, begin the following litany.)

Leader   Jesus, we believe in you. We want to follow you as the saints did. Help us to be like Agnes.

All   Help us to be like Agnes.

Leader   Help us to be like Joseph.

All   Help us to be like Joseph.

Leader (Continue naming as many of the saints mentioned by the children as you can recall and add to this list any other saints you want to pray to.)

Leader All you saints of God, all you who followed Jesus, help us to be saints, too. Amen.

All Help us to be saints, too. Amen.

(Now play the music and invite the children to process around the room several times as little saints of God.)

6 *The Sign of the Cross*

To Prepare   Using colored construction paper, help the children draw and cut out crosses. Have each print his or her name on the cross. Then invite all to sit in a circle on the floor, holding their crosses.

Leader   Children, look at the cross you have made. What is it really? Is it just a shape, like a letter of the alphabet? It looks very much like a "T" doesn't it? Is your cross just a shape like a square or a triangle, something that takes up a certain amount of space? Or does your cross mean something more than how it looks or feels? Does it stand for anything special?

(Allow the children to say what they think the cross means. Some may relate it to the cross of Jesus or the Sign of the Cross.)

Leader   Some of you knew that the cross is a special symbol for us Christians. It reminds us that Jesus has great love for us. He loved us so much that he gave his life for us. In memory of this we even use the cross in our prayers. We sign ourselves with it.

(Ask the children to touch the top of their crosses, then both sides and finally the bottom. Then demonstrate the Sign of the Cross, and how this gesture follows similar movements. If you are facing the group, be sure to sign yourself "in reverse," so that the children, imitating you, will sign themselves correctly. Then have them practice making the Sign of the Cross in a very reverent manner.)

Leader   We can take home the crosses we have made, and we should keep them in a special place. When we look at them they will remind us of Jesus. Even better, we can make the Sign of the Cross often through the day. When we do this we are telling God that we know we are not alone, and that we are doing all things in Jesus' name. Let us now pray together our special Christian sign.

All   In the name of the Father, and of the Son, and of the Holy Spirit. Amen.

(Encourage the children to share with family members both the crosses they made and the Sign of the Cross they "prayed.")

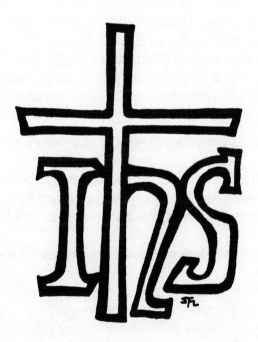

7   *Alleluia! Alleluia!*

To Prepare   Place a vase of flowers and a lit candle on the prayer table. Have available a large piece of poster paper and magic markers or crayons.

Leader   When something special—really special—happens to you, you shout for joy. Hooray, yippee, wow, fantastic. When grown-ups are really happy about something, they clap or cheer. These are natural things for people to do when they are happy or excited or both. The church also has an expression for special occasions. Does anyone know what it is? (Allow volunteers to guess.)

In the church we say Alleluia on special occasions. Alleluia means "Praise God." One very special time of joy in the church is the Easter season. During this time, our church says Alleluia over and over. We "praise God" over and over for the gift of Jesus' resurrection. The one who died on the cross is dead no more. He is risen, Alleluia!

Let us pray together now our own Easter prayer of joy.

Leader   After Jesus died on the cross, his body was placed in a tomb. (Ask all to repeat the following after you: "Jesus, we feel sad that this happened to you.")

All   Jesus, we feel sad that this happened to you.

Leader   When some women came to the tomb, the body of Jesus was not there. Two messengers in bright clothing told them: "Jesus is not here. He is risen." (Ask all to repeat the following. "Jesus, we feel glad about this good news.")

All   Jesus, we feel glad about this good news.

Leader   The women ran back to town to tell all the followers of

Jesus. "He is alive; he is risen; come to the tomb and see." Jesus, we feel like shouting for joy with the women. (Ask all to repeat: "Jesus is alive; he is risen.")

All   Jesus is alive; he is risen.

Leader   We praise you, God, for raising Jesus from the dead. It makes us happy that Jesus is alive and with us. Help us to believe in his resurrection and to keep on following him all of our lives. (Ask all to repeat: "We are so happy that Jesus is alive. Alleluia. Alleluia.")

All   We are so happy that Jesus is alive. Alleluia. Alleluia.

(Now invite each child to write the word Alleluia on the posterboard, with his or her name somewhere near it. Hang this class "poster" in a prominent place and leave it there during the Easter season.)

8 *The Spirit Has Been Sent*

To Prepare   Beforehand, prepare with the children brightly colored headbands (using construction paper) with a red flame attached to each. Practice with the children who will take the parts of Mary and John. Invite the children to sit around the room, as the friends of Jesus might have done.

Leader   After Jesus went back to heaven, his friends got together to pray. They asked God to show them how to tell people about Jesus and all that had happened to him. Mary, Jesus' mother, was with them.

Mary   I really miss Jesus. We're all going to miss him very much.

John   Well, Mary, Jesus said he would be with us forever. I guess he'll let us know what he meant sometime soon. What do you think he meant? How will he be with us?

Mary   I don't know, John. I feel sad, but at the same time, I'm excited. I feel that something great will happen soon to show us that Jesus keeps his word.

Leader   All of a sudden, without any warning, a loud noise filled the room. It sounded like the noise the wind makes when it's blowing really hard. The friends of Jesus felt the wind and they also saw little flames of fire spreading out all over the room. The flames settled above each one's head. (All now put on headbands.) At first they were afraid, but then they realized that this must be a sign of the Holy Spirit, the one sent by Jesus to be with them always.

John   This is the sign that Jesus promised. I feel sure of it, Mary. What a great day!

Mary   Yes, and we must go out now and tell everyone in the world about the gift we have received. Oh, how I hope that all people will want to share this gift. What a great day indeed!

Leader   Let us pray together now that we, too, may receive the gift of the Holy Spirit. Jesus, please give us your Spirit. (All repeat.)

All   Jesus, please give us your Spirit.

Leader   Help us to believe in you.

All   Help us to believe in you.

Leader   May your Holy Spirit be with us.

All   May your Holy Spirit be with us.

Leader   Forever and ever. Amen.

All   Forever and ever. Amen.

9 *Talking to God*

To Prepare	Have on hand pieces of 8 1/2"x11" paper and a pencil for each participant. Arrange on a prayer table a candle, a Bible, open to Matthew 6: 7-13, and four stand-up cards with these words on them: *Praise, Thanks, Asking,* and *Making Things Right.* There are parts for four readers, four pray-ers, and a leader.
Leader	Can we really talk to you, God, in an ordinary way? The problem for some of us is, we don't know what to say.
Reader One	When my mom or dad cooks something delicious, I say, "This is great!" When my friend builds a neat model, or puts together a hard puzzle, I say, "That's cool." Maybe I should tell God what I think about all the beautiful and great things I see every day.
First Pray-er	God, your world is incredible. You let flowers grow, and sun shine, and rain fall. The people you have made are totally awesome. They can smile and laugh and hurt and cry. They can think and create, and they can love one another. God, what you have made is great.
Reader Two	When someone does me a favor, I say, "Thanks." When my friend lets me borrow a special toy, I say, "Hey, thanks a lot." When my parents cook for me, or do laundry, or go to work to earn money, I know I should say thanks, but I forget sometimes. Maybe I should be telling God thanks, too, for all the big and little things that happen to me every day.
Second Pray-er	God, I had a good day today. I got all my work done in school and I didn't get in trouble once. I came home from school and there were cookies on the table, my favorite kind, and I didn't even have homework tonight. Supper was delicious and my favorite TV show was

great. And now, my bed is soft and warm. Thanks, God, thanks a lot.

Reader Three When I need something, like lunch money or extra money for ice cream, I ask my parents for it. When I need help with my homework, I ask my older brother to help me. When I am lonely or bored, I call up my friend and ask her to come over. Maybe I should ask God more often for the things I and other people need.

Third Pray-er God, I need your help all the time. It seems like as I get older, school work gets harder, and my parents want me to do more chores. And it takes longer and longer to do my homework. I need your help with friends, too, God. Michael thinks I don't like him when I play with Paul, and Jesse won't let me be on the kickball team unless I play every day. Please help me to know what to do, God.

Reader Four When I do something wrong, my parents want me to make up for it. Sometimes this means saying "I'm sorry" to someone, but it also means paying for things I break or lose, like a library book or a friend's toy. My father says it's important to make things right again. Maybe I should be making things right with God, too.

Fourth Pray-er God, I did something terrible last week. I lied to my teacher. She was yelling at me for not doing my homework and I told her that I was sick. I still had to stay in at recess and do the homework, but do I have to tell the teacher I lied? Anyway, I think she already knows. But I'm sorry that I did this, God, and I know that lying is wrong. Please help me to figure out how to make things right and please forgive me, God.

Leader (Now distribute papers and pencils and instruct all in the group to fold the paper in half horizontally and then in half again to form a "booklet.")

God, there are so many things to praise you for, so many good things in our lives. Help us to pray in praise. (Ask all to write a short prayer of praise on page one.)

God, there are so many things to thank you for, so much

that we receive every day. Help us to pray our thanks. (All write a thank-you prayer on page two.)

God, there are so many things we need help with, so many things to ask for other people and for our world. Help us to pray by asking. (All write a petition prayer on page three.)

God, there are so many times that we let others down, that we do things we know to be wrong. Help us to pray for forgiveness. (All write an "I'm sorry" prayer on page four.)

God, we offer you the prayers in these booklets. And we offer you now the prayer that Jesus taught us to pray.

(All recite the Our Father.)

FOR PRE-TEENS
AND TEENAGERS

10   *Ask and It Will Be Given*

To Prepare   The following brief service can be used at the beginning of class with any group of students. Gather around a prayer table on which is placed a lighted candle and a Bible (open to Luke 11:10-13). Give the two readers their parts beforehand so that they can practice reading them prayerfully.

Leader   (Invite all participants, with bowed heads and closed eyes, to be still and to quiet their thoughts. Allow approximately 60 seconds for this.)

Jesus, our brother and friend, we gather today as a class to learn about you and to understand how we might better follow you. Please guide us and teach us.

First Reader   Jesus, you told us in Scripture: "Ask and it will be given to you, search and you will find, knock and the door will be opened to you. The one who asks will receive; the one who is searching will always find, and the door is opened to those who knock....Thus, your heavenly Father will give the Holy Spirit to those who ask."

Second Reader   Jesus, please give each of us the courage today to ask, to search, to knock, and thus to receive your Spirit. Open our minds and hearts during this class that we might receive you, find you, and have the door opened to us.

Leader   Please respond "Amen" to the following: Those who ask will receive...

All   Amen.

Leader   Those who search will always find...

All   Amen.

Leader   Those who knock will have the door opened to them...

All   Amen.

Leader   Those who ask for the Holy Spirit will receive the Holy Spirit...

All   Amen.

Leader   We are now asking, God. Please answer our prayer in Jesus' name...

All   Amen.

11 *Advent Waiting*

To Prepare   Have on hand a large candle, small slips of paper 1"x2", pencils, magic tape, and a Bible (open to Psalm 131). As participants arrive, invite them to sit in a circle on the floor around the candle. Have someone light the candle.

Reader   O God, my heart isn't proud, nor do I look down on others. I don't busy myself with great things to impress others, nor with things beyond my reach. No, rather, I have stilled and quieted myself like a contented child, like a contented child on its mother's lap. I am at peace and I am waiting.

Listen people, this is my message: Rely on God, now and for always.

Leader   Let us now, in quiet and in peace, reflect on these words. (Allow two minutes for this.)

All of us are "waiting" in our lives, sometimes consciously, sometimes not. Some are waiting for an invitation, some are waiting for a job, some are waiting to get out of school, some are waiting to get into school. All of us spend time every day doing some form of waiting. In the psalm we listened to, the writer is also waiting. This person wants to be at peace and to be content with life. He or she knows that such peace and contentment comes from relying on God.

And so, as we wait in various ways in our lives, let us place our wants and needs in the hands of God. Remember the words of the psalmist. Listen people, this is my message: Rely on God, now and for always.

(Now invite participants to think of one thing they are particularly waiting for at this time. Ask them to write this out on one of the slips of paper. Since these will be read aloud, they should not be highly personal, and participants should not sign their names. Collect all the papers in a container, mix them up and have each person draw one out. When all the papers have been drawn, ask participants to take turns reading out the "wish" written on the paper. After each reads, have him or her tape the ends of the paper together, encircling it with the next piece. The united slips of paper will eventually form a finished chain. The completed chain should be placed around the lighted candle.)

Leader God, our loving parent, bless us as we wait together for the gifts we need. Help us to wait in peace and contentment for these things and for the coming of Jesus, your greatest gift to us.

All Amen.

12   *Come, Lord Jesus*

To Prepare   Make a large sign that reads: *Come, Lord Jesus.* Also write these words on individual cards for each participant. Place the large sign in a place visible to all, and put the small cards in a special container on the prayer table. Invite all to sit in a circle on the floor as they arrive.

Leader   On TV, the radio, and in our newspapers, people refer to this time as "28 shopping days left before Christmas." In the church we call this time "Advent." The church believes that the important thing about Christmas is the celebration of Jesus' birthday. We give presents to one another in memory of God's gift to us. God gave us Jesus to live among us and to guide us. So, it is only right that we stop and think: What is Christmas really about?

Reader One   Come, Lord Jesus, into our hearts. Help us to believe in you and to celebrate with you at Christmas.

Leader   Is Christmas about getting presents? Is it about decorating our homes and our Christmas trees? Is it about having school parties and parties with friends? Is Christmas about having relatives visit from out of town or having company for Christmas dinner?

Reader Two   Come, Lord Jesus, into our hearts. Help us to believe in you and to celebrate with you at Christmas.

Leader   All of the ways we celebrate Christmas are good, and we can and should enjoy them. But we have to ask ourselves: Is something missing from what we do? Do we know *why* we exchange gifts and decorate trees? Do we know *why* we gather with family and friends? Do we know *why* we have special parties?

Reader One Come, Lord Jesus, and help us to remember that you are the reason we celebrate Christmas. Help us to celebrate your birth.

Leader We do all these special activities because of the coming of Jesus. Jesus is the greatest gift God could ever have given us. Our gifts should remind us, our decorations should remind us, our parties and gatherings should remind us: Jesus is among us. Jesus is always with us. What great news!

Reader Two Come, Lord Jesus, and help us to remember that you are the reason we celebrate Christmas. Help us to celebrate your birth.

Leader To remind you that Jesus is the reason for Christmas, I have made each of you a special card. (Now call each person forward, in turn, to receive one of the cards. When all are back in the circle, continue.) Take this card home and put it in a place where you can see it in the days before Christmas. Let it remind you that Jesus is with you, and it is the gift of Jesus that you will celebrate at Christmas. Make this your prayer (ask all to repeat after you: "Come, Lord Jesus.")

All Come, Lord Jesus.

13 *The Way of the Cross*

To Prepare Set up 14 stops or stations throughout the room. At each of these, place a cardboard sign (numbered from one to 14), and on each sign draw a large black cross. In the center of the room, set up a prayer table on which is placed a large cross or crucifix and a lit candle. Pre-assign readers for the 14 stops or stations. As participants enter, invite them to sit in a semi-circle around the prayer table. Explain that you will be praying together a shortened version of the Stations of the Cross.

Leader Lord Jesus, we have gathered here to follow your path to Calvary. Help us to listen, to reflect, and to pray, believing that you are present, always with us, always loving us.

Reader One (at station one) All others can remain in one place or move from station to station—as the group decides.) Jesus is condemned. Jesus did and said only good things. His only concern was to introduce people to a new and better way of life. Yet, he upset the way things were. The leaders had him arrested and he was condemned to die. What must he have felt at that moment?

(Moment of silence)

Jesus, forgive us for the times that we, too, have condemned you.

Reader Two (at station two) Jesus carries his cross. Many of those in the crowd knew Jesus. They saw the cross being placed on his shoulders, and yet they didn't come forward. After all he had done, they did nothing. He must have felt totally alone and rejected.

(Moment of silence)

Jesus, forgive us for the times we walk away from the burdens of others.

Reader Three	Jesus falls the first time. Jesus fell as the soldiers pushed him forward. He fell in front of people who had followed him and in front of his own mother. How must he have felt; what was he thinking?

(Moment of silence)

Jesus, forgive us for the times we refuse to help others when they fall.

Reader Four	Jesus meets his mother. Mary loved Jesus so much. She wanted people to accept him, to believe him, and to love him as she did. But here she sees him suffering and humiliated. How must she have felt at that moment?

(Moment of silence)

Jesus, forgive us for the times we have not accepted you and believed in you.

Reader Five	Simon helps Jesus carry the cross. Poor Simon! Why was he the one forced to help with the cross? He was just passing by; he was minding his own business. What would people think? Did Simon, even for a moment, forget his own embarrassment and consider how Jesus felt?

(Moment of silence)

Jesus, forgive us for the times we refuse to consider the feelings of others.

Reader Six	Veronica wipes the face of Jesus. Veronica rushed forward with her towel. Her sympathy overcame her fear, and she wiped the blood and sweat from Jesus' face. Did she realize how dangerous that was? Did she care?

(Moment of silence)

Jesus, forgive us for the times we refuse to take risks for others.

Reader Seven	Jesus falls a second time. When Jesus fell again, he must have been extremely weak. He had lost a lot of blood, and the crowd was closing in on him. Was he feeling sorry for himself, or was he thinking of us?

(Moment of silence)

Jesus, forgive us when we fail to "be there" for our family and friends.

Reader Eight   The women weep for Jesus. The women wept for Jesus because he was obviously in pain. They were crying because there was nothing they could do but stand by and watch. Did any of them really feel sorry for Jesus? Did they realize that he was suffering for them?

(Moment of silence)

Jesus, forgive us for the times we forget how much you love us.

Reader Nine   Jesus falls for the third time. Jesus fell three times with the heavy cross on his shoulders. He could barely move and yet the soldiers roughly pulled him up. He was so weak; where did he get the courage to go on?

(Moment of silence)

Jesus, forgive us for the times we have been too afraid to do what's right.

Reader Ten   The soldiers tear off Jesus' clothes. Jesus was stripped in front of a whole crowd of people. He was undressed against his will. He was too weak to protest, and yet how humiliated he must have felt.

(Moment of silence)

Jesus, forgive us for the times we have selfishly humiliated others.

Reader Eleven   Jesus is nailed to the cross. Jesus was the victim of anger and jealousy; he had stirred up the people; and now ugly things were being done to him. As he felt the horrible pain of the nails in his hands and feet, what was he thinking about? Was he worried about himself—or about others?

(Moment of silence)

Jesus, forgive us for the times we refuse to forgive others.

Reader Twelve   Jesus dies on the cross. For three hours Jesus endured the pain of hanging on the cross. Yet, even as he hung there, he prayed for others: Father, forgive them, they don't know what they're doing. How could he have forgiven them? How does he forgive us?

(Moment of silence)

Jesus, forgive us for the many times we only think of ourselves.

Reader Thirteen   Jesus is taken down from the cross. Joseph of Arimathea, a secret follower of Jesus, came forward after Jesus had died. He dared to claim the body of a "criminal." What made him do it? Wasn't he afraid of being called a criminal, too?

(Moment of silence)

Jesus, forgive us for the times we walk away from people when they need us.

Reader Fourteen   Jesus is placed in the tomb. Jesus spent his public life preaching, healing, and guiding others. He talked about the kingdom of God and promised it to his followers. But in the end he was crucified and his body was placed in another's tomb. No friends or followers gathered around. Where were they? Where would we have been?

(Moment of silence)

Jesus, forgive us for our lack of faith. Teach us what it means to follow you.

Leader   (When all have returned to the circle) We know from Scripture that Jesus' story didn't end on Good Friday. Easter Sunday morning followed. "He is not here," God's messenger said; "he has been raised from the dead." As followers of Jesus, we can believe that rejection, loss, even death and dying, don't always lead to failure. We can move through these experiences toward resurrection—as Jesus did. Let us pray together now for the courage to accept our life experiences as Jesus accepted his. (Invite all to spend five minutes in silent prayer and reflection before leaving.)

14   *Seeking the Good News*

To Prepare   Have available ten plastic Easter eggs (the kind that can be opened), small pieces of paper, a pencil, blindfolds for half the group (handkerchiefs or old pieces of cloth will do), and a candle. Beforehand, carefully read one of the gospel accounts of the resurrection. Choose ten key words or phrases from this account that capture for you the essence of the story. Write one of these words or phrases on each of the ten slips of paper. Insert one paper in each egg, then close the eggs. Shortly before this service, hide the eggs in various places around the room.

At the beginning of the service, divide participants into pairs. Ask each pair to determine which partner is older. This one will wear the blindfold. After a starting signal, each sighted partner should guide his or her counterpart toward finding the hidden eggs, calling out verbal commands such as, "straight ahead," "to the left," etc. This should continue until each pair has found at least one of the eggs.

When all of the eggs have been collected, ask participants to guess what might be in them. Let them open them one at a time to read the word or phrase inside. Challenge the group to put the message together in the proper order. (Allow at least five minutes for this, if needed.)

Now invite participants to close their eyes and reflect on the following questions:

•In the activity of searching for the eggs, what was the significance of some of you being blind? Do you ever feel that you are sometimes searching in the dark for meaning?
•Some of you acted as guides in the activity. In your life-search, who are your guides?

•The words inside the eggs didn't mean much individually. Taken together, they represent one of the greatest mysteries of our faith. What does this message mean to you?

Leader As Christian people, we are called to offer life to one another, as Jesus offered life to us. We are all blind in some ways, and we need others who will lead us toward truth. And, we sometimes are the ones who must lead, even though we barely know the way. In the story of his resurrection, Jesus teaches us that we need not fear our blindness or our weakness. We will be strengthened by God as Jesus was. We, too, will be raised up.

Jesus, as we prepare for Easter, be with us. Guide us toward the truth and help us in our weakness.

(Now invite participants to pray spontaneous prayers of petition for the blessings and graces they need. Next light the candle and reflectively read the gospel story from which you drew the words or phrases. All exchange a sign of peace before leaving.)

15   *With Cries of Joy*

To Prepare   In a preceding class or session, assign each participant a country. (You might even have these written out on slips of paper to insure that they will be remembered.) Ask them to locate the country on a map and learn at least one fact about the people who live there. Countries you might assign are: Botswana, Mongolia, Finland, Libya, New Guinea, Guatemala, Uruguay, Brazil, Canada, Iceland, and Zaire. In a word, try to include a wide range of diverse cultures. On the day of the service, have the names of the assigned countries in a special container on the prayer table. Also place a candle on this table and a Bible (open to Psalm 46).

Leader   (Ask participants to repeat each of the following prayer phrases from Psalm 46 after you.)

All you peoples, clap your hands...
Shout to God with cries of joy...
Yell out praises to our God, yell out praises...
Spread the word...
God created all the earth...
God created all the peoples of the earth...
Amen. Alleluia...

Reader One   Let us now pray for all our brothers and sisters throughout the world. May our God give all of us love and understanding, for we are all God's children. East to west, north to south, all the world over, we are God's children. (The reader bows his or her head in silent prayer as a sign to participants to do the same.)

Reader Two   Who are the people of God? Where do they live and what do they do? Are they sometimes happy, sometimes sad? Do they go to school, have jobs? Do they relax and enjoy themselves? Who are the people of God?

(The leader now goes to the container on the prayer table and draws out a country. The person who was assigned this name comes forward and says something about the people there. Then the leader recites the following petition:)

For the people of ———————, let us pray to the Lord.

All Lord, hear our prayer.

(The leader repeats this process until all the country names have been used. If a person has forgotten their country, offer suggestions about the people there.)

Leader As we once again praise God, let us imagine that standing here with us are people from all the countries of the world. Close your eyes and picture one of these people. (Pause.) In your imagination, invite him or her to join us as we now pray: (Again, invite participants to repeat each line after you.)

All you peoples clap your hands...
Shout to God with cries of joy...
Yell out praises to our God, yell out praises...
Spread the word...
God created all the earth...
God created all the peoples of the earth.
Amen. Alleluia...

16 *We Profess Our Faith*

To Prepare Divide the group into two sections, a right section and a left section. Make copies of the following service for each participant. Place a large sign or poster in the front of the group that reads: *We Profess Our Faith*. Leave room on the poster for each participant to sign his or her name. Have colored markers available.

Leader When we gather for worship, we profess our faith by reciting the Nicene Creed. It has this name because it was put together long ago at the Council of Nicea by church leaders. These leaders listed all the things Christians believed. They started with God the Father and creation, then went on to God the Son, his life, death, and resurrection, and concluded with God the Holy Spirit. For centuries Christians have repeated this formula as a way of saying "yes" to their beliefs. Let us now join all the Christians who have gone before us as we together profess our faith.

Right Side We believe in one God, the Father, the Almighty, maker of heaven and earth, of all that is seen and unseen.

Left Side ...of all that is seen and unseen.

Right Side We believe in one Lord, Jesus Christ, the only son of God, eternally begotten of the Father, God from God, Light from Light, true God from true God.

Left Side Begotten not made, one in being with the Father, through him all things were made.

Right Side ...through him all things were made.

Left Side For us and for our salvation he came down from heaven.

Right Side By the power of the Holy Spirit he was born of the virgin Mary, and became man.

Left Side For our sake he was crucified under Pontius Pilate; he suffered, died, and was buried.

Right Side ...he suffered, died, and was buried.

Left Side On the third day he rose again in fulfillment of the scriptures; he ascended into heaven and is seated at the right hand of the Father.

Right Side He will come again in glory to judge the living and the dead, and his kingdom will have no end.

Left Side ...and his kingdom will have no end.

Right Side We believe in the Holy Spirit, the Lord, the giver of life, who proceeds from the Father and the Son. With the Father and the Son he is worshipped and glorified. He has spoken through the prophets.

Left Side ...he has spoken through the prophets.

Right Side We believe in one, holy, catholic, and apostolic Church.

Left Side We acknowledge one baptism for the forgiveness of sins.

Right Side We look for the resurrection of the dead, and the life of the world to come.

Left Side ...and the life of the world to come. Amen.

Right Side Amen.

Leader As a sign that we are believers, I invite you all to come forward now to write your names on this sign (poster).

(After all have signed the poster, spend several minutes in silent prayer.)

17 *God Is Light*

To Prepare	Make two large signs. On one, print the word *Light*; on the other, print the word *Darkness*. Then cut out 2"x2" squares of paper, two for each participant, and place these in a container (to be used during the service). Beforehand, place one of the signs on one side of the meeting space, and the other on the opposite side. Invite participants to sit in a circle on the floor.
Leader	This is the message that we have received from God's Word. God is Light, and no darkness can exist in God. The darkness is beginning to lift, and the true light is now shining in the world. Anyone who claims to be "in the light" and hates his brother or sister is, in fact, still in darkness. But the people who love their brothers and sisters live and move in the light and have no reason to stumble (1 John, chapter one).
Reader One	Who are our brothers and sisters?
Reader Two	The members of our family, the kids in our class, the people in our neighborhood, the citizens of our country, people from all the nations of the world, these are our brothers and sisters.
Reader One	Are they young as well as old, black as well as white? Are they healthy as well as sick, are they educated as well as uneducated? Are they Russian, or Spanish, or Greek, or African?
Reader Two	They are all these things. All the children of God, all over the earth, are our brothers and sisters.
	(Now ask everyone to come forward to take two slips of paper. On one, have them write a feeling toward others that they have actually felt, but that belongs in the

"darkness," for example, hate, jealousy, gossip, etc. On the other slip, ask them to write a feeling toward others that belongs in the "light," for example, kindness, courtesy, patience, etc. They shouldn't say these aloud, just write them. Also do this exercise yourself.)

Leader   Let us now go the the place of "darkness" and there leave our dark feelings behind. (Lead participants to the sign that says *Darkness* and place your "dark" slips beneath it.) Let us now go the the place of "light" and there leave our feelings that belong in the light.

(Lead them across to the other sign and there leave the "light" slips. Return to the circle. Ask the group which feelings they felt better about. Explain that though we all sometimes feel "dark" feelings, we can make a conscious choice not to act on those feelings. We can do this with Jesus' help.)

Let us pray. Jesus, what we wrote on these papers, we have actually felt in our hearts. Help us to always choose the light, even when we are tempted by the darkness. Please give us the light you lived by, so that we may love all others and not dwell in darkness. Guide us that we may walk in your light. Amen.

FOR CATECHISTS
AND OTHER
PARISH MINISTERS

18   *We Rejoice in Our Faith*

To Prepare   On a prayer table place a lighted candle, a Bible, a textbook, and a teacher's manual. (For other parish ministries, substitute symbols that represent those particular ministries.) Beforehand, type out or hand-write a verse card for each participant. These can be more or less elaborate. Copy or type onto each card a verse from the following service; for example: *May you understand the great power you have received*, or, *May God give you the spirit of wisdom.* Place these cards in a container on the prayer table.

Leader   (Read dramatically.)

Ever since I heard about your faith, I have not stopped giving thanks for you and remembering you in my prayers. I keep asking God to give you the spirit of wisdom and revelation, so that you may know God better. I pray also that the eyes of your heart may see what it is God is calling you to. And may you see the glorious inheritance that is planned for you and understand the great power you have received. This power is the same power that God used to raise Jesus from the dead and to place him above all created things. With Christ, we can now experience the fullness of God who fills up everything in every way (Ephesians 1:15-23).

(Allow a short time for silent reflection.)

Leader   (holding up the candle from the prayer table) See this light, a symbol of Christ. May the light of Christ fill your minds and hearts as you prepare to serve the church.

All   We welcome the light of Christ.

Leader   (holding up the Bible) See this book that contains the Word of God. May you share its wisdom and revelation with those you serve.

All   We welcome the Word of God.

Leader   (holding up the textbook) See this textbook that contains a message of faith. May you guide each person who uses it to greater knowledge and love of God.

All   We welcome this message of faith.

Leader: (holding up the manual) See this manual that contains guidelines for teaching the message of faith. May it lead you and those you teach to ever greater faith.

All   We welcome these guidelines for teaching the faith.

    (The leader now picks up the verse cards from the table and invites each person to come forward to receive his or her card and a blessing/prayer. For example, the leader might say the following:"_____, go forth in peace and rejoice in the faith you are about to share." After all have received a blessing, the following prayers of petition begin.)

Leader   For each of you, that you may understand your calling, experience the power of God, and appreciate your gifts. let us pray to the Lord...

All   Lord, hear our prayer.

    (The leader adds several petitions that apply directly to all present, and then invites participants to pray their own spontaneous petitions.)

Leader   It is with God's own power that we are called forth. It is only with God's gifts of wisdom and revelation that we can serve. God, our loving parent, guide and strengthen us, and above all, calm our fears as we go forth to proclaim the gospel. Watch over us and bless us.

All   Amen.

19   *Our Eyes See, Our Ears Hear*

To Prepare   Before this service, ask participants—in person or by mail—to bring to the service a small object that symbolizes God's presence for them. As they arrive, place these objects on a central prayer table on which there is a lit candle and a Bible (open to Matthew 13:10-17).

Leader   Let us begin our time of prayer with a reading from God's Word:

The disciples said to Jesus, "Why do you use parables when you teach?" Jesus answered, "The knowledge of the secrets of the kingdom of heaven has been given to you, not to everyone...I use parables because people look, but do not see, and they listen, but do not hear or understand. Remember what the prophet Isaiah said: 'This people will listen and listen, but not understand. They will look and look, but not see, because their minds are dull, and they have stopped up their ears and have closed their eyes. Otherwise, their eyes would see, their ears would hear, their minds would understand, and they would turn to me, and I would heal them.'

"As for you," Jesus continued, "how fortunate you are! Your eyes do see and your ears do hear. I assure you that many prophets and many of God's people wanted very much to see what you see, but they could not, and to hear what you hear, but they did not."

This is the Word of the Lord.

All   Thanks be to God.

First Reader   What is it that Jesus wants us to see? Is it that God's kingdom is already among us? And that there are signs pointing to it all around us?

Second Reader	What is it that Jesus wants us to hear? Is it the sounds of life in our created world, the voices of our brothers and sisters, the Word solemnly proclaimed at our liturgies?
First Reader	How fortunate we are. Jesus tells us that our signs and sacraments symbolize something beyond themselves. They point us to the presence of God, the kingdom of God.
Second Reader	How fortunate we are. Our eyes do see and our ears do hear the signs and sacraments of God's presence.
	(Invite participants to reflect silently about what God is saying to them through the symbol they brought with them. Then pray as follows.)
Leader	Jesus, guide us now as we share some of the signs of your presence among us. Open our hearts and minds to whatever it is you want us to see and hear more clearly this day.
	(Ask participants to come forward, in turn, and pick up their symbol from the prayer table. Facing the group and holding high the symbol, each should announce: "This is a sign of God's presence.")
All	Amen.
Leader	(After all have had a turn, go to the prayer table and pick up the Bible. Hold it high and announce the following: "This, too, is a sign of God's presence among us.")
All	Amen.

20   *Symbols of Our Service*

To Prepare   Set up a prayer space, on which is placed a candle, a Bible (open to John 13:4-9), a white towel, a basin or bowl, and as many small white cloths (cut-out 4"x4" squares) as there are members of the group.

Opening Song   Any appropriate recorded hymn with a service theme. Invite participants to sing along or to simply listen prayerfully and reflectively.

Leader   A reading from the Gospel of John (13:4-9):
Jesus rose from the supper table, took off his outer clothes, picked up a towel and fastened it around his waist. Then he poured water into the basin and began to wash the disciples' feet and to dry them with the towel around his waist. In this manner he came before Peter, who said to him: "You must never wash my feet!" Jesus answered, "Unless you let me wash you, you cannot share my lot."

"Then, please," Peter countered, "wash my hands and face as well."

This is the Word of the Lord.

All   Thanks be to God.

First Reader   Here we are, Lord, your followers, your friends. Your message to us is that as you have done, so we must do. How are we to serve your children? How are we to wash their feet?

Second Reader   When I take time to prepare lessons, though I'd rather be reading...when I enter that room full of lively children, though I feel insecure and sometimes even afraid...when I proclaim your Word and share my faith, though I feel unworthy...Is this washing their feet?

First Reader   Here we are, Lord, your followers, your friends. Your message to us is that as you have done, so we must do. How are we to serve your children? How are we to wash their feet?

Second Reader   When I come to teacher meetings, or Scripture study sessions, though I am tired from a day's work…when I attend a catechetical conference or a workshop, though my children and spouse would like me at home…when I volunteer for paraliturgies and field trips, though I have a long list of personal errands to do…Is this washing their feet?

First Reader   Here we are, Lord, your followers, your friends. Your message to us is that as you have done, so we must do. How are we to serve your children? How are we to wash their feet?

Leader   I invite you now to reflect on and pray about this question in silence. What is the answer closest to your own heart? (Allow approximately five minutes for this.)

First Reader   Here we are, Lord, your followers, your friends. Your message to us is that as you have done, so we must do. How are we to serve your children? How are we to wash their feet?

(Now invite participants to "pray aloud" ways that they might better serve those they teach. Begin the process in this way: Jesus, help us to be more patient in our teaching [more creative, to add more humor, etc.] When all have had a turn to name something, take the white cloths from the prayer table. Facing those present, present the "towels" one at a time in the following manner:)

Leader   _____, receive this cloth as a symbol of your service.

(After each presentation, all respond: "Amen.")

21 *We Are Spirit People*

To Prepare Arrange chairs in a circle and set up a prayer table in the center of the circle. On the table place a candle, a Bible (open to John 15:26-27), and an arrangement of spring flowers (if possible, one for each participant).

Opening Song Use any appropriate hymn, but preferably one that expresses Easter joy.

Leader We are spirit people. Our faith reveals that all around us and about us—truly even within us, the Spirit of Jesus is at work. Then, too, all those who have gone before us in faith are among us in spirit. The problem is, we rarely get in touch with this spirit world. We rarely exercise our ability to be spiritual people. Let us take time now to relax, and to focus in on the Spirit within us. (Allow five minutes for this. Invite participants to move elsewhere in the room if they so desire.)

Reader One Jesus said to his friends and followers: "When the Spirit of Truth comes, whom I will send to you, you will learn about me. And you must also testify, as the Spirit does, for you have been with me all along."

Reader Two "When the Spirit of Truth comes," Jesus promised, "he will guide you into all truth. The Spirit will speak for me and tell you what it is you are to do."

Leader When does your Spirit speak to us, Jesus? We never hear your voice. When does your Spirit tell us what to do? We never hear. We never hear.

Reader One Forgive us for the times we invite noise into our hearts and minds, and thus turn off your Spirit.

Leader When does your Spirit speak to us, Jesus? We never hear your voice. When does your Spirit tell us what to do? We never hear. We never hear.

Reader Two Forgive us for being too busy to listen, or too afraid to hear what you might be saying to us.

Leader When does your Spirit speak to us, Jesus? We never hear your voice. When does your Spirit tell us what to do? We never hear. We never hear.

(Now invite all present to answer this question in his or her own heart. Pause.)

Reader One The Easter season lasts 50 days. Easter is not over on Easter Sunday. Rather, in one sense, it just begins. With Jesus among us as risen Lord, for 50 days we move joyously toward the coming of the Spirit. During this special liturgical time, we should try to comprehend all the ways in which the Holy Spirit is speaking to us.

Reader Two Through all the people who cross our paths, through those we serve in the parish, through our times of prayer, through all the great and small things God has created, the Spirit of Jesus is speaking to us.

Leader Is it that your Spirit is always speaking to us, Jesus? We will try harder to hear your voice. Is it that your Spirit is always telling us what to do? We will try harder to hear. Yes, we will try harder to hear.

(If there are enough flowers for all participants, now invite each forward to receive a flower. Say to each the following words:)

Leader Receive this small reminder that the Spirit of Jesus is speaking to you.

All Amen.

22 *Caring for the Poor*

To Prepare The following prayer service incorporates principles from *Economic Justice For All*, a pastoral on the economy issued by the American bishops. It can be used with groups of catechists, teachers, and other parish ministers, as well as with high school groups. Prepare and distribute copies of the second half of this service (in which there are parts for "All") to all participants.

Leader *Economic Justice for All* is a letter from our bishops. It is a personal invitation to us to use the resources of our faith, the strength of our economy, and the opportunities of our democratic system to shape a society that protects the dignity and basic rights of our sisters and brothers in this land and around the world. This letter is long and it touches on complex issues, but the following six basic statements or themes are the heart and soul of it:

Reader One Our economy should be serving the needs of people, not the other way around.

Reader Two The gospel instructs us to "love our neighbor," but the present economic system encourages us to "love and advance ourselves."

Reader One All people have the right to make economic decisions and to reap economic benefits, but in our present economy only the rich and powerful are encouraged to exercise this right.

Reader Two We should be making economic choices that benefit the poor, the weak, the elderly—as well as ourselves.

Reader One All people have the fundamental right to life, food, clothing, shelter, medical care, education, and employment.

Reader Two Our government ought to take an important role in helping protect these rights for all its people.

Leader Through their letter, our bishops are inviting us to think about these questions and to try to find answers to them. This won't be easy. But we shouldn't be surprised if we find Christian social teaching to be demanding. The gospel itself is demanding, and we are always in need of conversion, of a change of heart, if we are to answer its call.

Reader One So, let us now together pray and reflect on our Christian call to "change our hearts" by using the words of our bishops from *Economic Justice for All*.

(Here, participants begin using the papers that you distributed.)

Leader We know that, at times, in order to remain truly a community of Jesus' disciples, we will have to say No to certain aspects of our culture, to certain trends, and ways of acting that are opposed to a life of faith, love, and justice.

All Jesus, our brother / give us the courage to say No / remembering that in this world / four million children under five / die each year from malnutrition and disease.

Reader Three It's hard to change how we act until we change our hearts. This is especially true for those of us who work away from home. Work so often seems unrelated to our Christian calling. From time to time, it's necessary to ask ourselves: With what care, human kindness, and justice do we conduct ourselves at work?

All Jesus, our brother / help us to conduct ourselves at work / with care, kindness, and justice / and let us not forget those who have no work / and those who constitute the "working poor."

Leader Some of us have positions of authority and some of us have wealth. It's necessary in these areas, too, to ask:

How will our economic decisions to buy, sell, invest, divest, hire or fire, serve human dignity and the common good?

All Jesus, our brother / help us to make decisions / that also serve the needs of others / and let us be aware / that in our great rush to invest and develop / we may be exploiting our natural resources / and damaging our environment beyond repair / and possibly polluting our air, land, and water.

Reader Three All of us, without exception, are influenced by our consumer society. Every time we watch TV, listen to the radio, or read a paper, we are bombarded by messages that invite us to buy and consume. Each in his or her own heart must ask: How can I develop a healthy detachment from things and avoid the temptation to assess who I am by what I have?

All Jesus, our brother / help us to learn that our call to be Christian / is worth more than all our possessions / and that none of us is justified in keeping / for our exclusive use / what we do not need / when others lack necessities.

Leader Our bishops are asking us to join with them in service to those in need; and to reach out personally to the hungry, to the homeless, to the poor and the powerless, and to the troubled and vulnerable. Each of us has to decide how best to do these things.

All Jesus, our brother / help us to reach out to those in need / and to believe that all people / especially the poor and powerless / are people with dignity./ Show us how to serve them.

Reader Three Our bishops conclude their letter with these words: "We believe that the Christian view of life, including economic life, can transform the lives of individuals, families, schools, and our whole culture. We believe that, with your prayer, reflection, service, and action, our economy can be shaped so that human dignity prospers and the human person is served. This is the unfinished work of our nation. This is the challenge of our faith."

All This is our unfinished work. This is our challenge. Amen.

23   *The Challenge of Peace*

To Prepare   Make copies of the following service for all participants. There are reading parts for eight readers and a leader. If possible, create a prayerful atmosphere by lighting a candle and semi-darkening the room. There will be several pauses for quiet reflection, so have paper and pencils available for any participants who want to write out their thoughts during these times. Also, if possible, have available a copy or copies of *The Challenge of Peace: God's Promise and Our Response* for those who might want to study it more fully.

Leader   "Faith does not insulate us from the challenges of life, rather it intensifies our desire to help solve them precisely in light of the Good News which has come to us in the person of Jesus, the Lord of History." These words are from the introduction to *The Challenge of Peace: God's Promise and Our Response*, a pastoral letter written by the American bishops. In this letter, the bishops dare to address the problems and complexities of war and peace. They do this humbly, knowing that what they say is not the final word; yet, they rely on scripture, tradition, and the living faith of all Christian people to support their concerns. Let us now reflect together prayerfully on some of the passages from this pastoral.

Reader One   At the center of the Christian teaching on peace and at the center of all Catholic social teaching are the transcendence of God and the dignity of the human person.

Reader Two   The human person is the clearest reflection of God's presence in the world; all of the church's work in pursuit of both justice and peace is designed to protect and promote the dignity of every person.

Reader One	For each person not only reflects God, but is the expression of God's creative work and the meaning of Christ's redemptive ministry.
Reader Two	Christians approach the problems of war and peace with fear and reverence. God is the Lord of life, and so each human life is sacred; modern warfare threatens the obliteration of human life on a previously unimaginable scale.
Leader	Let us pray. Lord God, you have made us with love and given us dignity and grace. How might we best respond to your call to be reflections of your love, dignity and grace. (Allow two minutes for silent reflection/prayer.)
Reader Three	Even a brief examination of war and peace in the Scriptures makes it clear that they do not provide us with detailed answers to the specifics of the questions we face today. They do not speak specifically of nuclear weapons, for these were beyond the imagination of the communities in which the Scriptures were formed.
Reader Four	The sacred texts do, however, provide us with urgent direction when we look at today's concrete realities. The fullness of eschatological peace remains before us in hope and yet the gift of peace is already ours in the reconciliation effected in Jesus Christ.
Reader Three	These two profoundly religious meanings of peace inform and influence all other meanings for Christians. Because we have been gifted with God's peace in the risen Christ, we are called to our own peace and to the making of peace in our world.
Reader Four	As disciples and as children of God, it is our task to seek ways in which to make the forgiveness, justice, mercy, and love of God visible in a world where violence and enmity are too often the norm.
Leader	Let us pray. Lord God, your word in Scripture challenges us to seek peace for ourselves and for our world. How might we best do this in our individual lives? (Allow two minutes for silent reflection/prayer.)

Reader Five	We live today in the midst of a cosmic drama; we possess a power which should never be used, but which might be used if we do not reverse our direction.
Reader Six	We live with nuclear weapons knowing we cannot afford to make one serious mistake. This fact dramatizes the precariousness of our position, politically, morally, and spiritually.
Reader Five	A prominent "sign of the times" today is a sharply increased awareness of the nuclear policy here and in other countries, which is unprecedented in its scope and depth.
Reader Six	Many forces are at work in this new evaluation, and we believe one of the crucial elements is the Gospel vision of peace. For many, the leaven of the Gospel and the light of the Holy Spirit create the decisive dimension.
Leader	Let us pray. Lord God, you know well that your people are part of a cosmic drama. How might we best and most effectively accept our roles as peacemakers in this drama? (Allow two minutes for silent reflection/ prayer.)
Reader Seven	Let us have the courage to believe in a bright future and in a God who wills it for us—not a perfect world, but a better one.
Reader Eight	The perfect world, we Christians believe, is beyond the horizon in an endless eternity where God will be all in all. But a better world is here for human hands and hearts and minds to make.
Reader Seven	For the community of the risen Christ is the beginning and end of all things. For all things were created through him and all things will return to the Father through him. It is our belief in the risen Christ which sustains us in confronting the awesome challenge of the nuclear arms race.
Reader Eight	The risen Christ is with us today in his word, sacraments, and spirit. He is the reason for our hope and

58

faith. Respecting our freedom, he does not solve our problems but sustains us as we take responsibility for the work of creation.

Leader Let us pray. Lord God, we believe that through Jesus you will indeed sustain us. Guide us as we reflect on how best to take responsibility for peace in our own hearts, in our families, in our communities, and in our world. Amen.

All Amen.

24 *Sow Justice, Reap Peace*

To Prepare Before participants arrive, arrange chairs in a circle and set up a prayer table in the center of the circle. On the table place a candle and a Bible (open to James 3:16-18). Behind the table (or somewhere visible) tape or hang a banner or sign that reads: *Jesus, we want to be just catechists.* Share the text in advance with the four readers.

Opening Song Use any appropriate hymn, but preferably one that develops the theme of "acting justly."

Leader (Read slowly and dramatically)

Where there is jealousy and selfishness,
   there is also disorder and every kind of evil.
But the wisdom from above is pure first of all;
   it is also peaceful, gentle, and friendly;
   it is full of compassion
   and it produces a harvest of good deeds;
   it is free from prejudice and hypocrisy.
And goodness is the harvest that is produced
   from the seeds of the peacemaker's plant.
This is the Word of the Lord.

All Thanks be to God.

Reader One What kind of catechist do I want to be? Let me see....First of all, I want to be fair. Everyone says that children respond well to a fair teacher. I want to be friendly, so that the children will really like me. And, I certainly want to be patient. It would be so embarassing to lose my temper just when the DRE walks by.

Reader Two I want to be well-prepared for each lesson, and never, absolutely never, go before the children unprepared. I want to be thorough, too. If I cover everything in the text, I'll feel better knowing that I have taught all the necessary information. I do want to be kind, but I also want to be firm. I would hate to be known as "the catechist with that wild class."

Reader Three Right from the start, I want to be businesslike with the children—so they won't fool around. So much time is lost when children aren't serious. I also want to be in touch with parents early on, so that I can contact those with "problem" children. I want my class to know that faith is a serious matter.

Reader Four I want to be the kind of catechist Jesus was. He reflected on Scripture to understand his role, and he relied on God to speak through him. He often prayed for strength to overcome obstacles. Above all, Jesus was gentle with children; he was more interested in blessing them and holding them than in teaching them. I'm not sure what this means in practice, but it's something I want to keep in mind.

(Now invite all present to reflect silently on the question: "What kind of catechist do I want to be?" Allow three minutes or so for this.)

Leader Jesus, our teacher, all of us have a picture in our minds of what it is you are calling us to be. But in Scripture you tell us that all our hopes and dreams, plans and schemes, methods and techniques will come to nothing unless we have Wisdom from above.

Reader One You are asking us first of all to be "pure" or clearsighted. Our goal is to reveal you and your gospel, not ourselves. You are asking us, too, to be peaceful, gentle, and friendly. At times we will have to rely on you for these gifts, especially when they don't come naturally to us.

Reader Two You are also asking us to be compassionate, so that we will want to understand and accept the children we teach, more than we personally want to be understood and accepted.

Reader Three Your Word assures us that Wisdom will produce in us a harvest of good deeds. What we sow, we will reap.

Reader Four Jesus, we need your help. Teach us how to love and care for your children so that we will indeed sow good things with them—and then reap peace in our classes. Amen.

All Amen.

25   *Prayers for the Year*

The following prayers can be used to begin catechist meetings, or they can be used privately by catechists and teachers as they begin their lesson preparations.

September   Jesus, here we are, beginning again. We ask you to bless each child we will be teaching. Speak through us that we may help them to grow in knowledge, in faith, and in love. Give us patience and understanding, so that through our service to them they may come to know you. Amen.

October   Jesus, some of the children in our classes are so cooperative and some are so exasperating! We are tempted to favor those who make our ministry easy. Yet we know that you have given us all of them to teach, and that you love each child as the unique person he or she is. Please share with us your wisdom, your patience and your love. Amen.

November   Jesus, this is the month for giving thanks. After some of our classes we feel anything but grateful! And yet, there are moments when we see the light of faith and understanding dawning on those we teach. Thank you for our call to be your messengers. Thank you for the children whose gifts as well as shortcomings are helping us to grow. Amen.

December   Jesus, you are the reason for all the excitement this month. Help us to remember this. The children get so carried away by the commercial aspects of Christmas. We want them to know you, and to understand that you are God's greatest gift to us. We celebrate Christmas in memory of this. Give us the courage to keep this message before those we teach. Amen.

January   Jesus, this is a bleak time for many of us. All of the holiday festivities are over and winter has settled in. All of the classes we have yet to teach loom before us. Help us to take them one step at a time, to see each one as an opportunity to put children in touch with you. Give us the courage to rededicate ourselves to helping them grow in faith and understanding. Help us to grow as well. Amen.

February   Jesus, can it be February already? Just when we thought winter would last forever, there have been some bright days on the horizon. The children seem to be getting it together. Some of them actually remember something from class to class. They seem more interested in praying, and they often ask questions that make sense. Help us to love them as you do. Help us to grow in love for you. Amen.

March   Jesus, we are learning a lot about ourselves these days. We realize how often we try to control what's going on in the minds and hearts of the children we teach. We want to take personal credit for what they know—or don't know. We're learning that we have to step back, to let you guide them—at their own pace. This is hard for us, so very hard. Give us patience and understanding. Amen.

April   Jesus, at last another chance to witness some of nature's incredible miracles. The flowers and plants that were "dead" are alive again. And this is the month to focus on the new life you experienced when you were raised from death. Easter is a wonderful season. Please help us to convey some of its beauty and wonder to those we teach. Raise them up, Jesus, from the distractions all around them, and help them to believe. Help us to believe, too. Amen.

May   Jesus, this is the month dedicated to your mother, Mary. How fitting this is. May is a lovely and gracious month. We're feeling happier about our teaching, maybe because it's winding down. But we have learned some important lessons this year, and we hope the children have too. Watch over them this summer as they continue to grow and develop as people. Give them the gift of faith and help them to remember that you are with them. Help us to remember, too. Amen.

FOR PARENTS
AND FAMILY GROUPS

26 *Listening to God*

To Prepare Arrange chairs in a semi-circle and set up a prayer table in the center. On it place a candle, an open Bible, and a bowl. Type out a shortened version of each of the Scripture passages used in this prayer service. Cut these into strips—enough for each participant—and fold them up. Place them in the bowl on the prayer table. Have paper and pencils available for each participant. Distribute these as they arrive.

Opening Song Use any appropriate hymn, but preferably one that refers to being still and listening to God.

Leader The following passages from Scripture point to our need as Christians to listen and to be open and present to God in prayer. Feel free to write down any words or phrases that particularly "speak" to you. (Now read the passages dramatically, pausing slightly after each.)

Be still and know that I am God (Psalm 46).

Speak Lord, your servant is listening (1 Samuel 3:10).

The Spirit of Truth will guide you toward everything that is true (John 14:16).

We do not know how to pray as worthy children of God, but the Spirit within us is actually praying for us in those agonizing longings that never find words (Romans 8:26).

At every turn life links us to the Lord. In life or death, we are in the hands of the Lord (Romans 14:7).

Leader Look at what you have written. What words or phrases appealed to you? Spend some time now reflecting, and writing if you wish, about how you might better relate to God in prayer. (Invite participants to move elsewhere in the room if they feel uncomfortable in the circle. Allow a full ten minutes for this reflection/writing time. Then invite everyone back into the circle.)

Reader   The Scripture passages we have heard and reflected upon all invite us to stillness. All of us need to give stillness a chance. We have to learn to pause, to stop being busy, to simply be still. By quieting ourselves we momentarily stop the distractions of our noisy world, and we are able to acknowledge that God is with us, within us, speaking to us.

Reader Two   Please pray the following words after me:

Be still and know that I am God…
Speak, Lord, your servant is listening…
The Spirit of Truth is guiding me…
The Spirit within me is praying…
At every turn life links me to the Lord…

Leader   We have prayed together about prayer itself, how it is important for us to pray, and important for us to pray with our children. As a reminder of God's invitation to us to be still and listen, I invite you to come forward now to receive a message for your continued reflection. (Hold the bowl as participants, one by one, take a folded slip.)

Leader   (After all have read their slips) God, our loving parent, thank you for these messages from your Word. May they strengthen us as we try to pray, and may they encourage us to share our faith with our children. We ask this through Jesus, our brother and friend.

All   Amen.

27 *The Light Shines On*

To Prepare   Darken the room and light a single candle. Beside the candle place a Bible (open to John 1:1-5), and any other items that symbolize Advent for this group.

Opening Song   Any appropriate Advent song, preferably one the participants know well.

Leader   Before the world was created, the Word already existed; the Word was with God, the same as God. From the very beginning, the Word was with God. Through him God made all things; not one thing in all creation was made without him. The Word has life in himself, and this life brought light to us. The light shines in the darkness and the darkness has never put it out (John 1:1-5).

(Invite participants to reflect on the following questions. Read them slowly and dramatically).

•How do you feel when you are alone in the dark? (pause)
•Look at the light of the candle. How do you feel about this light? (pause)
•Consider for a moment that John calls Jesus "light," the light that shines in our darkness. Close your eyes and think of Jesus in this way. (pause)
•John also says the darkness has never put out Jesus' light. How do you feel knowing that Jesus is always with you, always "light" in your darkness? (pause)

Leader   The liturgical season of Advent comes at the darkest time of the year. But our faith assures us that Jesus is the light of the world, a light that darkness has not overcome. This is our joy and our consolation, and this is the message of Christmas. This is the message we are called to share with our children.

Prayer Leader   Jesus, light of the world, help us to believe in the gift of your presence.

All   Please give us the light of faith.

Prayer Leader   Jesus, light of the world, help us to trust in the gift of your presence.

All   Please give us the light of trust.

Prayer Leader   Jesus, light of the world, help us to love you, present in one another.

All   Please give us the light of love.

(Now invite participants to spend five minutes in silence. At the end of this reflection/prayer time, ask all present to stand. Then invite each person to come forward, one at a time, for the following blessing.)

Leader   (Place your hand on each person's shoulder.) May Jesus, the light of the world, dispel your darkness. May he light your way during Advent.

All   (After each individual blesssing) May you always live in the light.

(When all have received their blessings, sing together, "This Little Light of Mine.")

28 *Celebrating the Seasons*

To Prepare Have available paper and pencils for all participants. On the prayer table place a Bible (open to Psalm 148), an empty container, and a stand-up card that reads: *All you seasons, bless the Lord.* Beforehand, make copies of the discussion questions for each family group.

Reader (Very dramatically read this adaptation of Psalm 148.)

Alleluia!
Let the heavens praise Yahweh:
Praise God, heavenly heights,
Praise God, sun and moon,
Praise God, all you shining stars.
All created things, praise the name of Yahweh,
At whose command you were created.
Let the earth praise Yahweh:
Sea monsters and all the deeps,
Fire and hail, snow and mist,
Storm winds that fulfill God's command.
Mountains and hills,
Orchards and forests,
Wild beasts and all tame animals,
All you snakes and birds,
All of you,
All created things,
Praise Yahweh,
For God's name alone is exalted
Above heaven and earth.
Alleluia! Alleluia!

Leader All of the created things we have called upon in this prayer are dependent upon the earth's changes. We call these changes seasons. Indeed, the seasons determine whether ice and snow or orchards and forests praise God. Nature's changes can be violent or they can be subtle. They can alter our way of life or barely affect it. They can offer us beauty and grandeur or struggle and challenge. In all these ways nature reveals to us the power and presence of God. I invite you now to enter into the mystery of the seasons. Reflect together and discuss this mystery using the following questions (hand out copies of these questions):

•Do you change with the seasons? In what ways?
•What is your favorite season? In what ways does it "speak" to you?
•What is your least favorite season? What struggles does it present?
•What do the seasons tell you about God?

(Invite families to discuss and/or write out their answers. Distribute paper and pencils to all. Allow five minutes for this reflection/discussion.)

Leader I invite you now to write down your family's strongest impression about the seasons—as a prayer. You can express wonder, serenity, anger, struggle, joy, sorrow, whatever emotion the seasons evoke in you. When you have completed your family prayer, place it in the container on the prayer table.

(Again, allow sufficient time for this. When all have placed their papers in the container, continue.)

Reader Yahweh, our God, you give us the seasons. May they praise you, and may we praise you through them. Accept our summer praise: for sunshine, for lakes and all bodies of water, for crops growing in the fields, for all your summer gifts, we thank you.

All For all your summer gifts, we thank you.

Leader Accept our autumn praise: for changing colors, for frost, for acorns falling, for crops harvested, for all your autumn gifts, we thank you.

All For all your autumn gifts, we thank you.

Reader Accept our winter praise: for cold and ice, for snow and wind, for the brown earth awaiting rebirth, for all your winter gifts, we thank you.

All   For all your winter gifts, we thank you.

Leader   Accept our spring praise: for budding flowers and new grass, for warm days and cool nights, for the rebirth that witnesses resurrection, for all your spring gifts, we thank you.

All   For all your spring gifts, we thank you.

Reader   (Go now to the container and, facing the group, lift it high.)

Leader   Yahweh, our God, the God of summer, fall, winter, and spring, accept our prayers. Accept our praise and our pleading, our expressions of joy, and our words of sorrow. Just as our Mother Earth changes and renews, so let us change and renew. With all created things, we praise your name. Amen. Alleluia.

All   Amen. Alleluia.

29   *We Are Called By Name*

To Prepare   Place the following objects on a prayer table at the front of the room: a white candle, a basin or bowl of water, and a white cloth (if possible, one of the baptismal cloths your parish uses). Prepare beforehand for each participant a small verse card that reads: *I have called you by name.* Also beforehand, hang in a visible place a sign or banner that reads: *God has called us by name.* As participants enter, hand each a copy of this service.

Leader   After his resurrection (before he was taken up to heaven), Jesus spoke these words to his followers:

Reader   You will receive power when the Holy Spirit comes upon you; then you are to be my witnesses in Jerusalem, throughout Judea and Samaria, yes, even to the ends of the earth.

Leader   When we were baptized, we received this promised Spirit, the Holy Spirit, the Spirit of Jesus himself. At that moment we were one with all those who witness to the presence of Jesus in our world.

Reader   At the moment of our baptism, we (or our parents or godparents for us) publicly expressed our belief that we belong to God. We accepted the waters of baptism as a sign of the way we would be living, the Christian way.

Leader   At that moment we received a lighted a candle as a sign that we would let our light shine in the darkness—the light of our faith in Jesus.

Reader   At that moment, too, we were given a new garment to wear as a sign that we would imitate Jesus, or as Saint Paul expresses it, we promised to "put on Christ" throughout our lives.

Leader	At the moment of our baptism, God called each of us by name to be a child of God, to be one with Jesus in the family of faith called church.
Reader	When we bring a child to this family of faith, we often forget that we, too, were once brought forward. We, too, were washed in the waters of forgiveness. We, too, once pledged our faith and received our call to be witnesses of Jesus. We, too, were called by name to be lights to our world. Let us now pray together as we recall our baptismal gifts.
Right Side	We have been baptized in the name of the Father...
Left Side	God, you have called us by name. We belong to you.
Right Side	We have been baptized in the name of the Son...
Left Side	God, you have given us your light. We will let it shine.
Right Side	We have been baptized in the name of the Holy Spirit...
Left Side	God, you have robed us in glory. We will "put on Christ."
Right Side	We have been baptized in the name of the Father, and of the Son, and of the Holy Spirit...
Left Side	God, you have given us new life in Christ. We will follow Jesus.
All	We will be witnesses, as Jesus commanded us to be. We will proclaim his name, even to the ends of the earth.
Leader	I invite each of you now to come forward to receive a sign of your baptismal pledge. (As each person is handed his or her card, say the following:——————————, God has called you by name. When all have received a card, continue: We have been made one family through the waters of our baptism. Let us now pray the words that Jesus taught us....)

(All recite the Our Father.)

30   *In Memory of Jesus*

To Prepare   On a center table place a loaf of bread and a container of grape juice (or wine if the group is old enough). Have available small paper cups for the sharing of the wine. Other items such as a candle, a Bible, and a vase of flowers can be placed on the table. Invite participants to sit on the floor or on chairs in a semi-circle around the table.

Leader   We are gathered here to remember the gifts that Jesus has given us. Among the many gifts we have received are the bread and wine that Jesus shared with his friends at the Last Supper. This was not ordinary bread and it was not ordinary wine. Through the sharing of this food and drink the followers of Jesus were challenged to remember him, to keep in their minds and hearts all that he had told them, and above all, to remember what he had done for them.

Today, we continue the tradition of sharing the bread and wine. At Mass, these gifts are blessed and consecrated in a particular manner by the priest. Our faith tells us that during Mass Jesus is actually present in the bread and wine. However, we don't have to wait for the celebration of Mass to remember Jesus. Even in our homes and classes we can remember him by sharing our faith and by sharing the gifts of bread and wine. That's what we are about to do now.

Reader One   As they were eating, Jesus took some bread, and when he had said the blessing, he broke it and gave it to them. "Take this," he said; "this is my body." Then he took a cup, and when he had returned thanks, he gave it to them, and they all drank from it. Then he said to them, "This is my blood, the blood of the covenant, which is to be poured out for many. Do these things in memory of me."

Reader Two   Every time we break the bread and drink the wine together at Mass we do it in memory of Jesus. But we can also remember Jesus at other times when we gather together in faith. In particular, we can remember that we have been called to love one another in the same way that Jesus loved us. Let us reflect silently for a moment about what this means in our daily lives. (Allow a minute or so for this.)

Side One   We have gathered here now to worship and to remember.

Side Two   Jesus, in this sharing, help us to recall your words, "Love one another as I have loved you."

Leader   (Invite participants to come forward one at a time to take a piece of bread. Break off pieces as they come forward, and say to each: "Take this bread, and let it remind you that Jesus is among us.")

(Next pour the juice or wine into the paper cups and invite all to come forward to receive it, one at a time. Say to each: "Take this wine and let it remind you that Jesus loved us so much he gave his life for us.")

Leader   (After all have received the bread and wine) Believing that Jesus is among us, let us pray for those we especially love and care for...

Reader One   For all our sisters and brothers around the world, that we may live in peace and harmony, let us pray to the Lord...

All   Lord Jesus, hear our prayer.

Reader Two   For all our families and friends, near and far, that God will watch over them and bless them, let us pray to the Lord...

All   Lord Jesus, hear our prayer.

Reader One   For all those in our parish family who are preparing to receive the eucharist for the first time, that they may experience peace and joy, let us pray to the Lord...

All   Lord Jesus, hear our prayer.

Leader   (Invite all present to now offer spontaneous petitions. When all have prayed, continue as follows:) In memory of Jesus, let us pray as he taught us. Our Father, who art in heaven. . . .

Leader   Let us now share the greeting of peace that Jesus gave his followers on Easter morning: "Peace be with you."

(All now exchange a sign of peace.)

31   *Searching for Peace*

To Prepare   Make a large poster (or banner) on which is printed the following: *Peace and Forgiveness*. On the prayer table, place a candle, a Bible (open to John 20:19-22), and a small card for each participant, which contains the words: *Peace Be With You*. Have available paper and pencils.

Reader One   In the evening on the first day of the week, the doors were closed in the room where the disciples were, for fear of the Jews. Jesus came and stood among them. He said to them, "Peace be with you," and showed them his hands and his side. The disciples were filled with joy when they saw the Lord, and he said to them again, "Peace be with you." Then he said, "As the Father sent me, so I am sending you." After saying this he breathed on them and said, "Receive the Holy Spirit. Whose sins you forgive shall be forgiven them."

This is the Word of the Lord.

All   Thanks be to God.

Reader Two   It's hard to imagine that the closest followers of Jesus were huddled in fear. They had spent a great deal of time with Jesus, listening to him, watching him, learning from him. Could they have so soon forgotten all that Jesus taught them?

Reader One   Lord Jesus, your followers were hiding and afraid, and they had been with you all along. What about us? How are we to follow you when your closest friends could not? And yet, after you "breathed on them" they regained the courage to try again. You gave them the gift of your Holy Spirit. Indeed, your Spirit has been given to us, too, and is among us, even here, even now, as we gather together to reflect on the meaning of the peace and reconciliation you offer us and our children.

Reader Two   Jesus, our friend, as we struggle to grow as Christian people and to teach our children Christian values, please help us to be aware of your Spirit within us. Our faith is weak and we are often afraid because we do not know your Spirit. Give us peace, your own peace, for which we are constantly searching. Forgive us for the times that we will surely fail, and strengthen us when we do, to get up and try again.

Reader One   When we were baptized, we received your Holy Spirit. When we received the eucharist and the sacrament of reconciliation, we were reminded that even in our weakness you are present. You are always offering us love and forgiveness. When we were confirmed we renewed the promises that were made for us at baptism. Indeed, your spirit, Jesus, has been with us in all the steps we have taken, and is among us now.

(Invite participants to now spend five minutes in silent prayer. Explain that paper and pencils are available for those who want to write out their prayers/reflections. After the silent time, suggest that each person pray aloud one prayer of petition for forgiveness and peace. Begin the process yourself. Be sure to include a prayer of petition for the children in the parish who are preparing to receive the sacrament of reconciliation for the first time.)

Leader   (After the prayers of petition) Jesus hears our prayers. He is aware of our fears and our struggles. He is anxious to share with us the gift of his peace. I invite each of you to come forward now to receive a reminder of this. (As you hand each person a card, say the words: "Peace be with you." When all have received a card and this blessing, invite everyone to exchange a greeting of peace. Encourage parents to repeat this blessing at home with their children, especially with those who are preparing for first reconciliation. Suggest that they make a peace banner and a "Peace be with you" card with their children.)

32   *Come, Holy Spirit*

To Prepare   Have paper and pencils available for each participant. On the prayer table, place a Bible (open to Acts 2:1-12).

Leader   Imagine for just a moment a work place or a school that has no spirit. What would it be like to be there many hours a day? (brief pause)

Now imagine a work place or school that has plenty of spirit. What would it be like to be there? (brief pause)

(Spend time with participants discussing these two images. Then continue.)

Leader   It would be safe to say that the followers of Jesus had no "spirit" before Pentecost. They were literally spiritless. They were hiding in the Upper Room, afraid, unwilling to be recognized as followers of Jesus. They no longer had courage because Jesus was not with them. In your imagination, place yourself there among them. Who would be beside you? What would you be saying? How would you feel? Excited? Afraid? Just waiting? (Lengthy pause)

Reader   When the day of Pentecost arrived, they were all together in the Upper Room. Suddenly there was a sound from heaven like the rushing of a violent wind, and it filled the whole house where they were seated. Before their eyes appeared tongues like flames, which separated off and settled above their heads. They were all filled with the Holy Spirit and began to speak in different languages as the Spirit gave them power to proclaim the Good News.

Leader   At that moment the followers of Jesus were once again a spirited people. They felt alive and courageous, and they remembered the promise from Jesus that he would send the Spirit, his Spirit, to dwell among them. In your imagination, place yourself again among the followers. What are you saying now? Who is with you? How do you feel? Still frightened? Enthusiastic? Courageous? (lengthy pause)

(Distribute pieces of paper and pencils to participants. First ask them to think about the coming of the Holy Spirit, perhaps by recalling their own confirmation or that of an acquaintance. If they could re-live that moment, what gift would they most want from the Holy Spirit? Or, (knowing what they know now) what would they need from the Spirit to live a Christian life? Ask them to print this one gift or quality on their papers. Note: They are not to put their names on these papers. Collect the papers, mix them up, and then ask each person in the group to pick a slip.)

Leader   Just as the Spirit of Jesus transformed the frightened apostles into courageous Christians, and gifted them with wisdom, understanding, courage, peace, patience, and joy, so, too, the Spirit will transform us. Together, let us pray that we may be ready to receive the gifts the Spirit has prepared for us.

(Now, in turn, each participant prays aloud, using the slip of paper he or she has chosen. Their prayers should take this form:)

Spirit of Jesus, give us the gift of (name the gift on the slip of paper) that we may be followers of Jesus.

(When all have prayed, spend a few moments in silent prayer, especially remembering those in the parish who are preparing for the sacrament of confirmation.)